Ripley's— ®

Believe It or Not!

TIME WARP

The past and present collide!

PUBLISHING

Executive Vice President, Intellectual Property Norm Deska
Senior Director of Publishing   Amanda Joiner

Editorial Director   Carrie Bolin
Editor   Jessica Firpi
Designer   Mary Eakin
Researcher   James Proud
Proofreader   Rachel Paul
Fact checker   Jordie R. Orlando
Reprographics   *POST LLC

Published by Ripley Publishing 2018

10 9 8 7 6 5 4 3 2 1

ISBN 978-1-60991-239-0

Library of Congress Control Number: 2018945621

Manufactured in China in May 2018.
First Printing

For more information regarding permission, contact:
VP Intellectual Property
Ripley Entertainment Inc.
7576 Kingspointe Parkway
Suite 188
Orlando, Florida 32819
Email: publishing@ripleys.com
www.ripleys.com/books

WARNING
Some of the stunts and activities are undertaken by
experts and should not be attempted by anyone
without adequate training and supervision.

PUBLISHER'S NOTE
While every effort has been made to verify the
accuracy of the entries in this book, the Publisher
cannot be held responsible for any errors contained
in the work. They would be glad to receive any
information from readers.

Ripley's Believe It or Not!®

TIME WARP

The past and present collide!

Ripley PUBLISHING®

a Jim Pattison Company

A light bulb at a fire department in California has been operational since

1901—

the year Australia became a country.

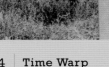

Beijing, China,

had existed for **300** years by the time **Ancient Rome** was founded.

Woolly mammoths
existed for centuries after the
Egyptian pyramids were built.

Charles Darwin and
Abraham Lincoln
were born on the same day—February 12,

1809.

The **fax machine** was patented

five days

after the first major **wagon** train

set off down the **Oregon Trail** in

1843.

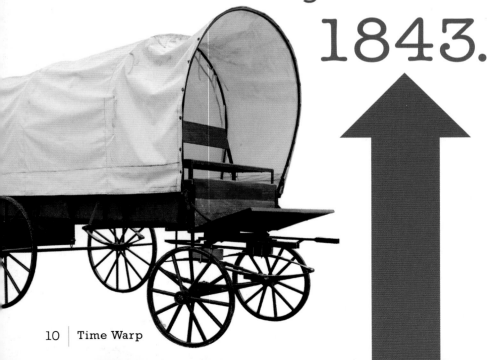

The LEGO company was founded the year the George Washington U.S. quarter went into circulation.

1932

The Samurai

fought their last battle the year of the first

The book *I, Robot*
was published in

1950,

the same year

Disney's *Cinderella*
was released.

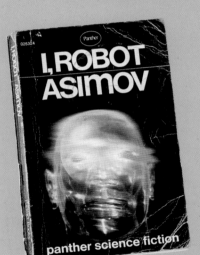

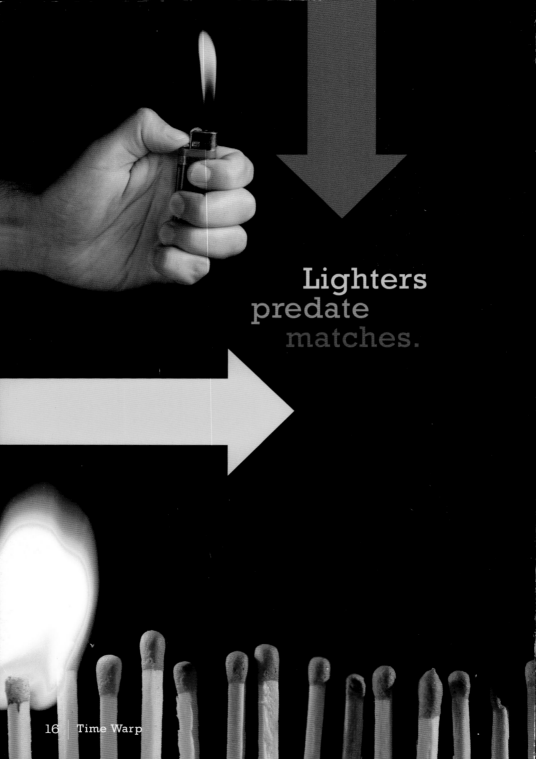

Lighters predate matches.

Samuel Seymour

of Maryland witnessed the

assassination of
Abraham Lincoln

and talked about it on television in

1956.

Grand Central station

has been around

54 years

longer than the Aztec Empire.

GRAND C
TERMI

The **first email** was sent during **the Vietnam War**, in **1971.**

Between when we discovered Pluto (1930) and declassified it as a planet (2006), Pluto still has not completed an orbit around the sun.

Jupiter

Mars

Earth

Venus

Mercury

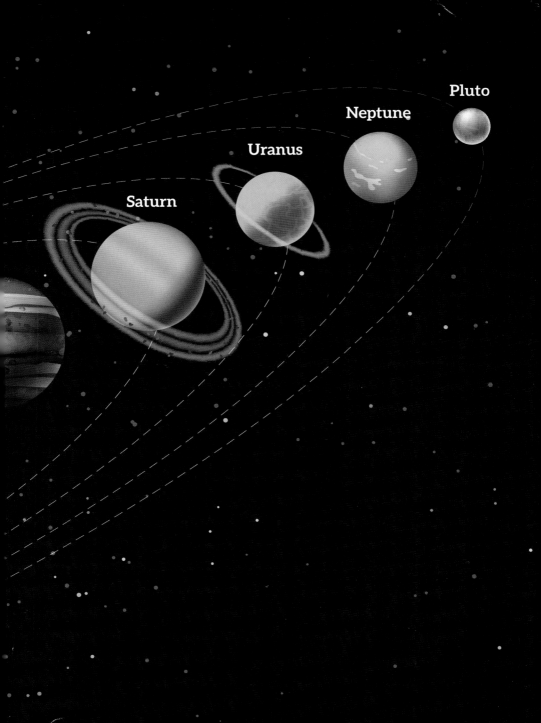

Saturn

Uranus

Neptune

Pluto

The first contact lenses were created in

1887.

The Russians safely landed a spacecraft on the Moon for the first time the same year that *Star Trek* premiered.

Beauvais Cathedral in France
is still unfinished, despite construction starting
at the time of the Crusades, almost

800
years ago!

A **clam** discovered in

2006

is thought to have been alive
at the same time as

Christopher Columbus.

Channing Tatum
is the same age as
Macaulay Culkin.

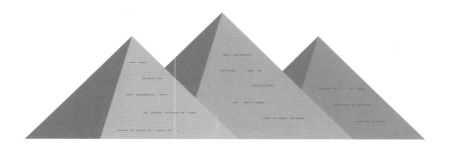

The Great Pyramid of Giza was the tallest structure in the world for almost

4,000 years.

Fairy tale author
Hans Christian Andersen
was alive during the American
Civil War.

Telephone pioneer
Alexander Graham Bell

and Thomas Edison

were born within a month of each other in

1847.

Oreos were introduced the year...

the Republic of China

was established.

1912

The painter **Vincent Van Gogh** was born **one year** before **Louis Vuitton** was founded in **1854.**

The world's **oldest living land animal,** Jonathan the giant tortoise, has lived through the last **39** of the **45** U.S. presidents.

Sumo wrestling
became a professional sport
in Japan around the same time...

Shakespeare's
Hamlet
was first performed.

The **Atlanta Braves**
were founded the year that
Germany became a country in
1871.

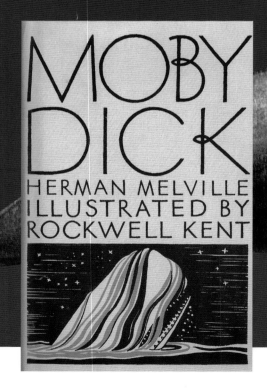

MOBY DICK

HERMAN MELVILLE
ILLUSTRATED BY
ROCKWELL KENT

There are **whales** alive today who were born before **Herman Melville** wrote *Moby Dick.*

The **Eiffel Tower** opened the same year **Nintendo** was founded as a **card company.**

Superman is older than World War II.
He first appeared in
June 1938.

Louisiana
became a U.S. state
a few months before
the waltz was introduced
in English ballrooms.

People were racing horses in the **Kentucky Derby** for more than

20 years

before the first modern **Olympic Games** in Athens in

1896.

We made it to the **Moon** only

65 years after the
Wright brothers
invented human flight.

The last **witchcraft trial**
to take place in the United Kingdom was during
World War II, in

1944.

Sherlock Holmes
first appeared in print less than two months after
the **elevator** was patented in

1887.

The **Himalayan Kingdom** of Bhutan finally allowed television in

1999!

When the **Colgate** toothpaste company was founded, **Thomas Jefferson** was president.

The **Chinese** invented toilet paper
100
years before
Columbus landed
in America.

Less than **40** years separates the
first microchip and **Google**.

The Moon landing and the TV debut of *Scooby-Doo, Where Are You!* both happened in

1969.

Pocahontas was born in

1596,

one year before Shakespeare's
Romeo and Juliet
was published.

THE
MOST EX=
cellent and lamentable
Tragedie, of Romeo
and *Iuliet*,

*Newly corrected, augmented, and
amended:*

As it hath bene sundry times publiquely acted, by the
right Honourable the Lord Chamberlaine
his Seruants.

LONDON
Printed by Thomas Creede, for Cuthbert Burby, and are to
be sold at his shop neare the Exchange.
1 5 9 9.

The **passenger pigeon** went extinct the year World War I began.

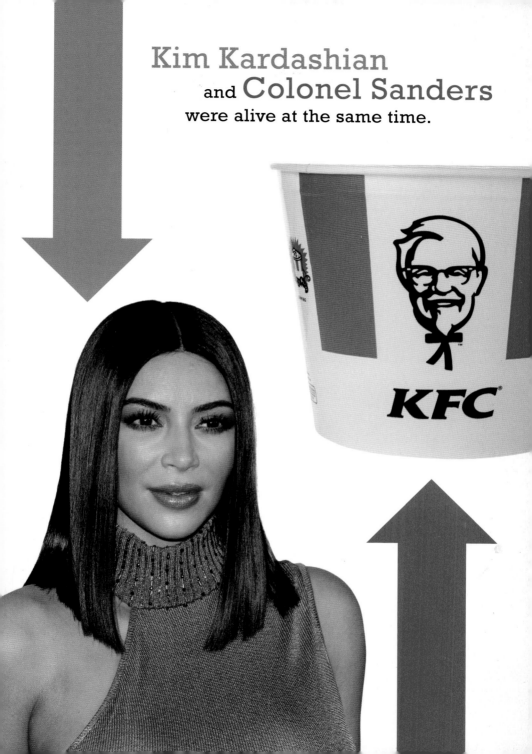

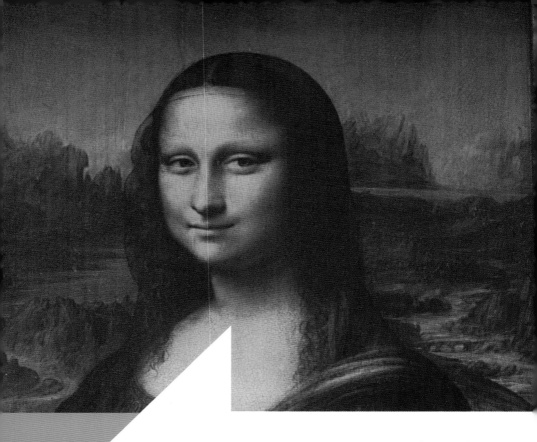

It took Leonardo Da Vinci up to **16** years to finish painting the **Mona Lisa...**

while it took
Michelangelo just **4** years
to paint the ceiling of the
Sistine Chapel.

The first Internet domain was registered the same year that *Back to the Future* premiered.

1985

China had writing paper around

800 years

before it appeared in Europe.

105 A.D. vs. 900s A.D.

Jellyfish existed

350 million years

before dinosaurs.

The state of Mississippi did not officially **abolish slavery** until **February**

2013.

When the **Spanish** first made contact, the **Inca Empire** numbered

12 million people,

more than the entire Spanish empire at the time.

The **Converse All-Star basketball shoe** was introduced in

1917–

32 years

before the NBA existed.

Shakespeare
was writing plays when the
Jamestown colony
was established in Virginia in
1607.

Sewing needles, rope,

boats, and the flute were all invented
thousands
of years before the wheel.

The Viking **Leif Erikson** landed in North America almost # 500 years before **Columbus** did.

The fifth actor to portray James Bond, **Pierce Brosnan,** is the same age as James Bond——he was born the year the first book was published.

Star Wars was released

May 1977...

France's **last guillotine**
beheading took place less than
4 months later.

The **telephone**
was patented the same year
that **sardines** were first canned
in Maine.

- -

American alligators
walked the Earth
at the same time as the
T. rex.

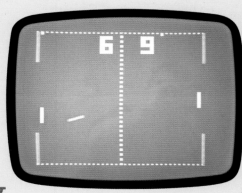

Elvis Presley
lived long enough to play
console computer games.

In **1971,**
it rained in an area of the
Atacama Desert, Chile,
for the first time in
400 years.

Pixar's *Toy Story 3*

was released the same day the

last execution by firing squad

happened in the

United States.

Pablo Picasso, J. R. R. Tolkien, and Bruce Lee all died in...

1973.

The game of bingo was introduced to North America the same year the Wall Street market crashed.

1929

STOCK MARKET CRASH AHEAD

The oldest living tree was growing when Stonehenge was being built—more than 5,000 years ago!

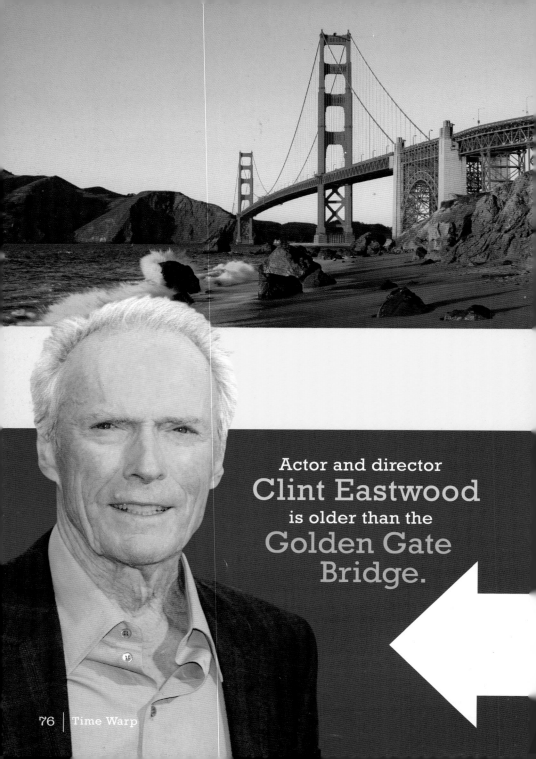

Actor and director
Clint Eastwood
is older than the
**Golden Gate
Bridge.**

Helen Keller was alive for the first Super Bowl ever.

Thomas Jefferson's handwritten French fry recipe predates cookbook French fry recipes by half a century.

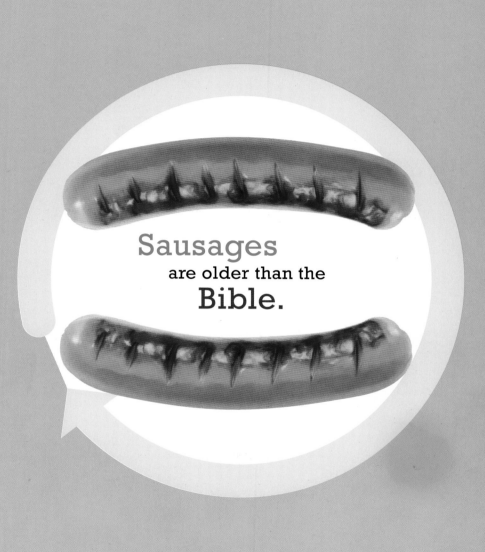

The Canadians started celebrating
Thanksgiving
42 years
before the pilgrims
arrived in America.

Silent movie star **Charlie Chaplin** lived long enough to see the release of the home PC in **1977.**

Canada became a country in

1867

but completed its independence
114 years later.

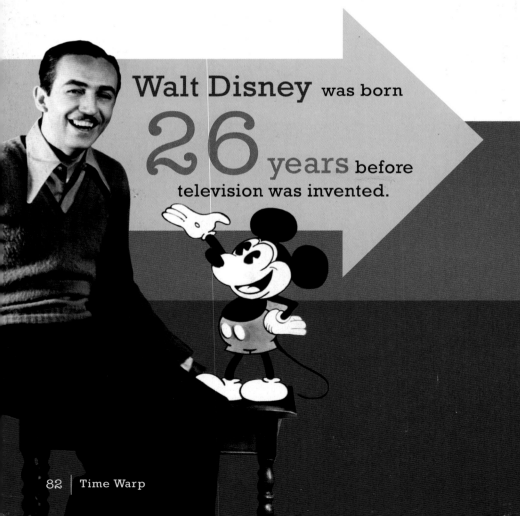

Walt Disney was born

26 years before
television was invented.

When the **Louvre Museum** in Paris opened, the United States was just

17 years old.

The **Stegosaurus** and the T. rex
never coexisted. They are separated by about

85 million years.

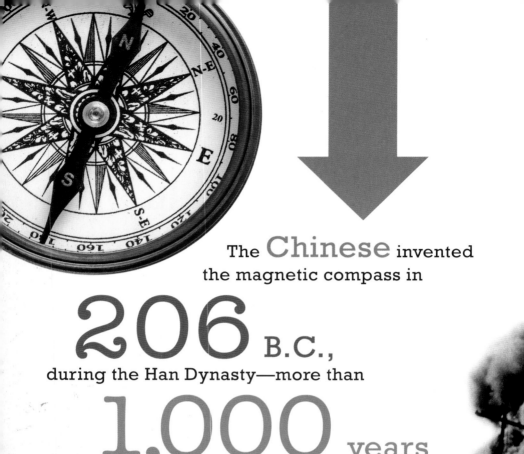

The **Chinese** invented the magnetic compass in

206 B.C.,

during the Han Dynasty—more than

1,000 years

before compasses appeared in western Europe.

The first digital computer was built the same year as the attack on Pearl Harbor in 1941.

The **tin can** was invented

48 years

before the
can opener.

1810/1858

The first human to human blood transfusion took place

151 years

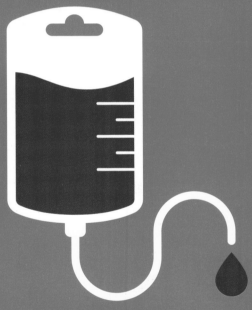

after the first animal to human transfusion.
1818 vs. 1667

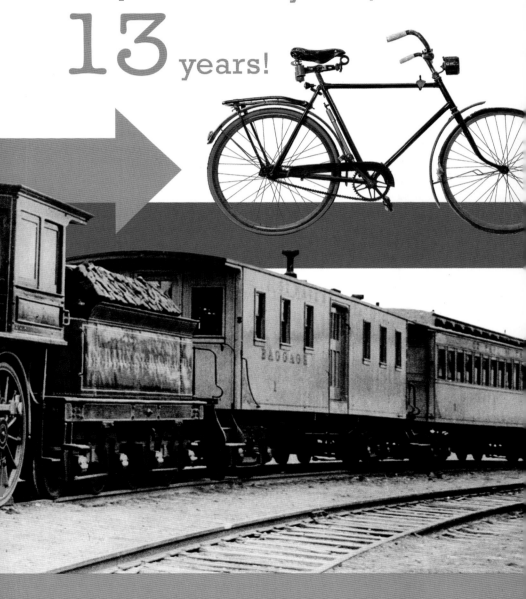

The **steam train** predated the **bicycle** by

13 years!

The last surviving **American Civil War veteran** lived to see **color television** in

1953.

Cleopatra lived closer in time to the building of the **first Pizza Hut** than the building of the **Egyptian pyramids.**

Both **John Adams** and **Thomas Jefferson** died on July 4,

1826—

exactly **50 years** after the adoption of the Declaration of Independence.

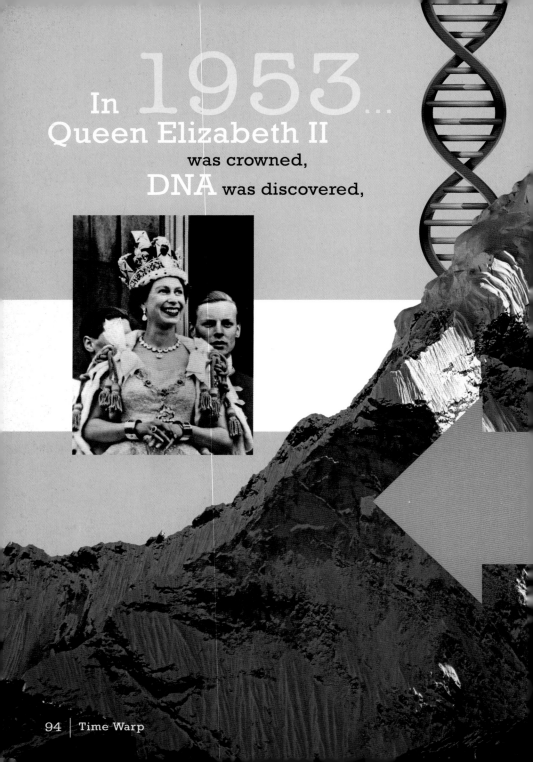

In 1953...
Queen Elizabeth II
was crowned,
DNA was discovered,

the first **James Bond** book was published, and climbers reached the summit of **Mount Everest** for the first time.

Civil rights heroine Rosa Parks
lived long enough to watch

YouTube.

Sliced bread
was invented in

1928,
35 years
after the electric toaster.

Marilyn Monroe and
Queen Elizabeth II
were born within three months of each other in...

1926.

The word "scientist" was not invented until

1834,

more than 100 years after the death of Sir Isaac Newton.

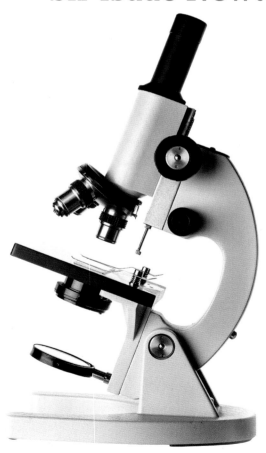

Macy's department store
was founded
before Italy became a country.

- -

The first-ever **Porsche** car, made in

1900,
was electric.

"O.M.G." was first used in a letter to **Winston Churchill** during World War I, in 1917.

- -

The first sighting of the **Loch Ness monster** was in the year **565.**

The **second sighting** of the mythical monster was not for another

1,368 years!

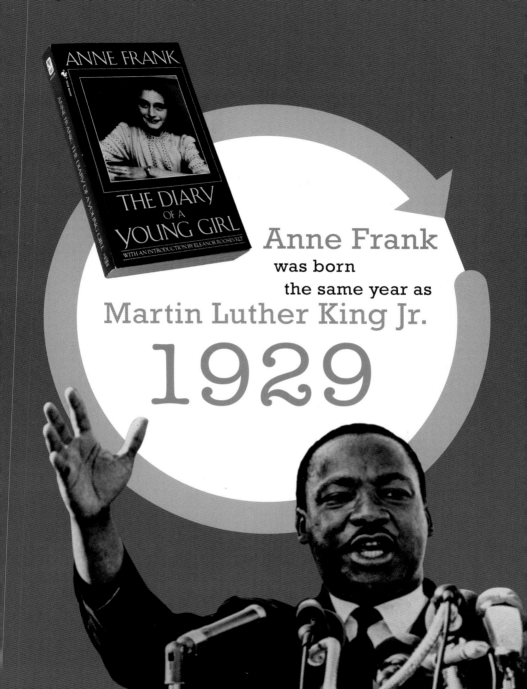

The first known mechanical alarm clock
was invented the same year the
U.S. Constitution was created in
1787.

The **first McDonald's**
opened its doors on May 15, 1940.

Two days later,
Nazi Germany
invaded France.

Soda was invented in

1767,

while Mozart was alive.

People have been saying
"God bless you"
after sneezes for more than

1,400
years!

The piano was invented less than

10 years after the

Salem witch trials.

The **modern smartphone** has more computing power than all of **NASA** had when it put astronauts on the **Moon.**

1911

The computer company IBM was founded the **same year** the first explorer reached the South Pole.

- -

Beethoven was 20 when Mozart died in 1791.

Mahatma Gandhi
was assassinated the year
NASCAR
was founded—**1948.**

The first woman member
of the U.S. Congress
began her first term

before
women had the right to vote.

1916/1920

There have been

426 more years

of **gladiator competitions** in Rome than years the **United States** has been a country.

Michael Jackson, Prince, and Madonna were all born in 1958.

The **car** was invented before the game of **basketball**.

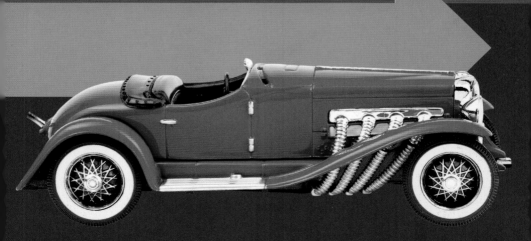

Women were excluded from the
Olympics track and field until
1928,
the same year Amelia Earhart
flew across the Atlantic.

HAMMOND·Y

DEPARTMENT OF COMMERCE

BUREAU OF AIR COMMERCE

Emilio Palma
of Argentina was the
first person ever born in
Antarctica—he only turns

40 in

2018!

When *The Simpsons* first aired,

the Soviet Union still existed.

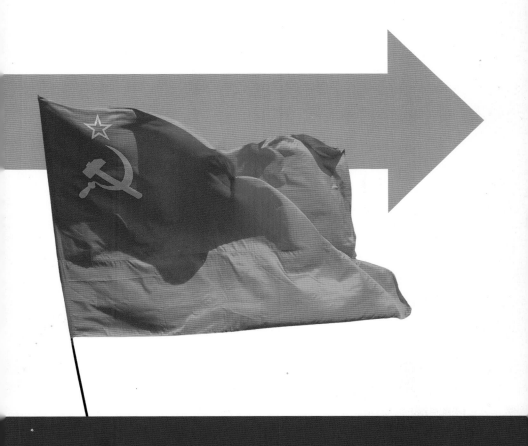

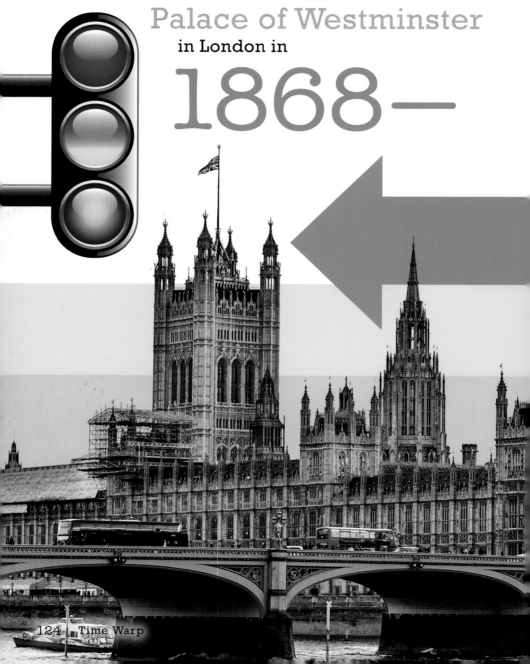

The **first traffic signals** were installed outside the Palace of Westminster in London in

1868—

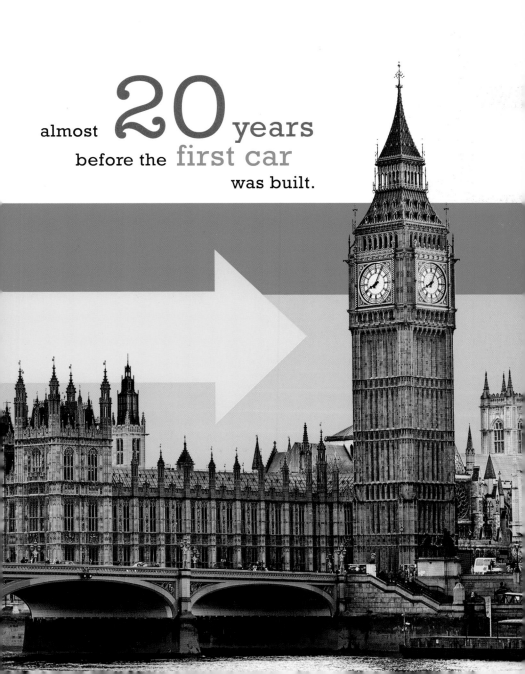

almost **20** years
before the first car
was built.

Oxford University
is older than Spain—by almost
400
years!

1096/1469

The vacuum cleaner
was invented the same year
Abraham Lincoln
was elected president in

1860.

Sabre-tooth
tigers
were still around when humans
first began farming

11,000 years ago.

The **Beatles**
released their first single in

1962,
the same year

Native Australians
got the right to vote
in federal elections.

BALLOT BOX

The first **flushing toilet**
was invented during the time of
Shakespeare in

1596.

When New York City was founded, the dodo still existed.

In **1886,**
Jacob's Pharmacy in
Atlanta, Georgia, sold
Coca-Cola
for the first time and
the Statue of Liberty
was dedicated in New York.

J. D. Salinger,

author of *The Catcher in the Rye*, lived long enough to read books on a Kindle.

Teddy Roosevelt witnessed **Abraham Lincoln's** funeral procession in

1865.

Mickey Mouse debuted the same year **clip-on ties** were designed.

1889

The jukebox was invented the year **Adolf Hitler** was born.

There are Greenland sharks
alive today that are older than the
United States.

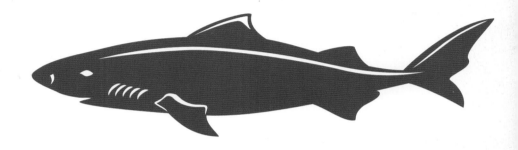

The first documented emoticons,

:-) and :-(

were posted on
Carnegie Mellon University
Bulletin Board System just five years after the first
color computer was released in 1977.

The first known use of the

@ symbol was in

1536—

the same year
Henry VIII executed
Anne Boleyn.

When Apple was founded in

1976,

Spain was still a dictatorship.

Confucius, Buddha,
and Pythagoras
were all alive at the same time in the

5th

century B.C.

The **Brooklyn Bridge** is older than

London's Tower Bridge
by **11** years.

The last surviving widow of a
U.S. Civil War veteran died in
2004!

- -

The modern **sewing machine**
was invented five years before
the **safety pin.**

1844 vs. 1849

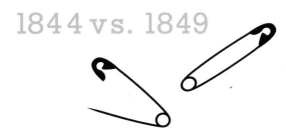

The current population of
New York City is greater than
that of **Earth**

10,000 years ago.

LEONARDO DiCAPRIO   KATE WINSLET

NOTHING ON EARTH
COULD COME BETWEEN THEM.

JAMES CAMERON FILM

TITANIC

FROM THE DIRECTOR OF 'ALIENS', 'T2' AND 'TRUE L

The movie *Titanic* is **34** minutes longer than it took the actual ship to sink.

Acknowledgments

Cover Design by Mary Eakin; **14** (b) Alpha Historica/Alamy Stock Photo, (ct) North Wind Picture Archives/Alamy Stock Photo, (cb) Glasshouse Images/Alamy Stock Photo; **15** (l) Chris Howes/Wild Places Photography/Alamy Stock Photo, (r) Moviestore collection Ltd/Alamy Stock Photo; **23** Photo 12/Alamy Stock Photo; **26** (t) Sabena Jane Blackbird/Alamy Stock Photo; **27** (r) Moviestore collection Ltd/Alamy Stock Photo; **29** (t) CBW/Alamy Stock Photo; **30** Sueddeutsche Zeitung Photo/Alamy Stock Photo; **31** David Cole/Alamy Stock Photo; **34-35** Simon Benjamin/Alamy Stock Photo; **38-39** WILDLIFE GmbH/Alamy Stock Photo; **38** (c) Heritage Image Partnership Ltd/Alamy Stock Photo; **40** (l) Shady Lewis/Alamy Stock Photo; **41** (t) carlos cardetas/Alamy Stock Photo; **51** (b) WENN Ltd/Alamy Stock Photo; **52** (b) Moviestore collection Ltd/Alamy Stock Photo; **53** (l) Chronicle/Alamy Stock Photo, (r) Ian Dagnall/Alamy Stock Photo; **56** Chad Ehlers/Alamy Stock Photo; **58** The Advertising Archives/Alamy Stock Photo; **61** imageBROKER/Alamy Stock Photo; **63** (r) Lou-Foto/Alamy Stock Photo; **65** (l) Rod Collins/Alamy Stock Photo, (r) Collection Christophel/Alamy Stock Photo; **67** Enrique RAmos/Alamy Stock Photo; **69** (t) INTERFOTO/Alamy Stock Photo, (b) ScreenProd/Photononstop/Alamy Stock Photo; **71** Photo 12/Alamy Stock Photo; **72-73** (dp) ScreenProd/Photononstop/Alamy Stock Photo; **72** (bl) Guillem Lopez/Alamy Stock Photo, (br) ScotStock/Alamy Stock Photo; **76** (t) Sydney Alford/Alamy Stock Photo; **77** (bkg) Chronicle/Alamy Stock Photo; **81** (t) INTERFOTO/Alamy Stock Photo, (b) Photo 12/Alamy Stock Photo; **82** Ronald Grant Archive/Alamy Stock Photo; **94** (l) Pictorial Press Ltd/Alamy Stock Photo; **95** (t) AF archive/Alamy Stock Photo; **96** (b) World History Archive/Alamy Stock Photo; **98** Bettmann/Contributor via Getty Images; **99** Max Mumby/Indigo/Getty Images; **103** (t) CBW/Alamy Stock Photo, (b) Glasshouse Images/Alamy Stock Photo; **114** (r) Lebrecht Music and Arts Photo Library/Alamy Stock Photo; **118** (tl) sjvinyl/Alamy Stock Photo, (tr) AF archive/Alamy Stock Photo, (b) CBW/Alamy Stock Photo; **122** AF archive/Alamy Stock Photo; **128** (t) Marc Tielemans/Alamy Stock Photo; **132** (l) ZUMA Press, Inc./Alamy Stock Photo, (r) Martin Williams/Alamy Stock Photo; **133** (l) WALT DISNEY/Ronald Grant Archive/Alamy Stock Photo

Key: t = top, b = bottom, c = center, l = left, r = right, dp = double page, bkg = background

All other photos are from Shutterstock.com

Every attempt has been made to acknowledge correctly and contact copyright holders, and we apologize in advance for any unintentional errors or omissions, which will be corrected in future editions.

Stop by our website daily for new stories, photos, contests, and more!

www.ripleys.com

 /RipleysBelieveItOrNot

 @Ripleys

 youtube.com/Ripleys

 @RipleysBelieveItorNot